Mel Bay's
FUN WITH THE BANJO

by Mel Bay

This book was created to help you have fun with the *banjo*. It will provide enjoyment and satisfaction to anyone desiring to play — so pick up your *banjo* and *have fun!*

This book is available either by itself or packaged with a companion audio and/or video recording. If you have purchased the book only, you may wish to purchase the recordings separately. The publisher strongly recommends using a recording along with the text to assure accuracy of interpretation and make learning easier and more enjoyable.

CD Contents

1. Introduction {:31}
2. Positioning {:51}
3. Tuning {2:04}
4. Positioning of the Pick {:36}
5. Time Signatures: 4/4 Time {:29}
6. Time Signatures: 3/4 Time {:20}
7. Time Signatures: 2/4 Time {:16}
8. The G7 Chord {1:03}
9. First Song Intro Exercises {:41}
10. Long, Long Ago {:41}
11. Down in the Valley {:48}
12. Skip to My Lou {:37}
13. Buffalo Gals {:35}
14. Oh, My Darling Clementine {:53}
15. The F Chord: 4/4 Time {:20}
16. The F Chord: 3/4 Time {:23}
17. The Blue Tail Fly {:37}
18. On Top of Old Smoky {:57}
19. The Marines Hymn {:53}
20. There Is a Tavern in the Town {1:12}
21. The D7 Chord & Exercise {:19}
22. The D7 Chord: 4/4 Time {:36}
23. The D7 Chord: 3/4 Time {:23}
24. The D7 Chord: 2/4 Time {:29}
25. Our Boys Will Shine Tonight {:33}
26. The G Chord {:12}
27. The G Chord: 4/4 Time {:20}
28. The G Chord: 4/4 Time {:30}
29. The Old Grey Mare {:45}
30. She'll Be Coming Round the Mountain {:31}
31. Hand Me Down My Walking Cane {:33}
32. Red River Valley {:42}
33. 3 New Chords {:15}
34. Fun With Chords in "C": 3/4 Time {:23}
35. Fun With Chords in "C": 4/4 Time {:26}
36. More Fun With Chords in "G": 3/4 Time {:24}
37. More Fun With Chords in "G": 4/4 Time {:26}
38. Home on the Range {1:07}
39. I've Been Working on the Railroad {1:02}
40. In the Evening by the Moonlight {:42}
41. The D Chord & Exercises {:18}
42. The D Chord: 4/4 Time {:21}
43. The D Chord: 3/4 Time {:18}
44. The D Chord: 4/4 Time {:31}
45. Darling Nellie Gray {1:35}
46. My Bonnie {:57}
47. Little Annie Rooney {:57}
48. Oh Susanna {:45}
49. Good Night Ladies {:46}
50. Further Study Information {:55}

1 2 3 4 5 6 7 8 9 0

Visit us on the Web at www.melbay.com — E-mail us at email@melbay.com

TUNING THE BANJO

The five open strings of the banjo will be of the same pitch as the five notes shown in the illustration of the piano keyboard.

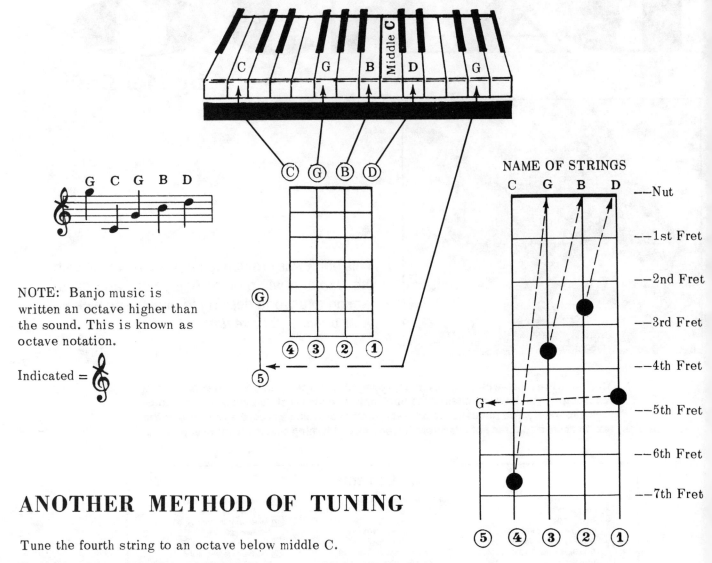

NOTE: Banjo music is written an octave higher than the sound. This is known as octave notation.

Indicated =

ANOTHER METHOD OF TUNING

Tune the fourth string to an octave below middle C.

Press the finger behind the 7th-Fret of the C - string and tune the 3rd or G string until it sounds the same pitch as the tone produced on the seventh Fret of the C-String.

Press the finger behind the fourth Fret of the 3rd string and tune the second or B-String until it sounds the same pitch as tone produced.

Press the finger behind the third Fret of the second string and tune the first string until it sounds exactly the same as the tone produced.

The 5th string sounds the same as the tone produced by placing the finger behind the fifth string of the first string.

PITCH PIPES

May be obtained and will produce the pitch of each string when blown into.

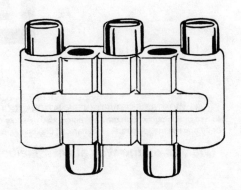

The Correct Way To Hold The Banjo

This Is the Pick

Hold it in

this manner ⟶

firmly between the

thumb and first finger.

Use a medium

soft pick.

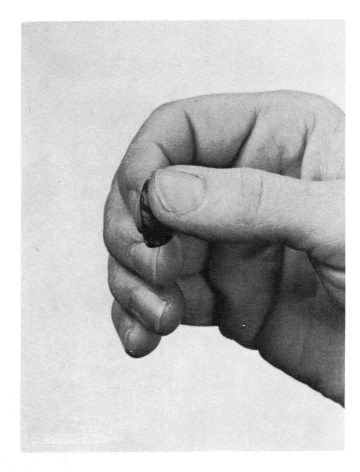

THE LEFT HAND

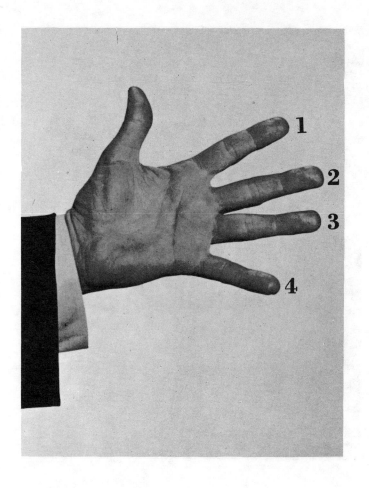

Practice
holding
the Banjo
in this
manner.

Keep palm
of the hand
from the
neck of the
instrument.

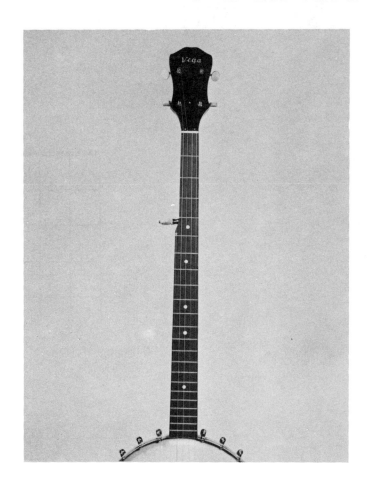

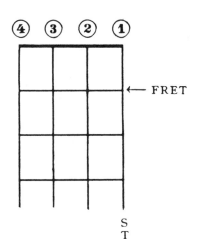

← FRET

S
T
R
I
N
G

The vertical lines are the strings.

The horizontal lines are the frets.

The encircled numbers are the number of the strings.

= 5th String (open)

Striking the Strings

with the fingers

with the pick

OUR FIRST CHORD

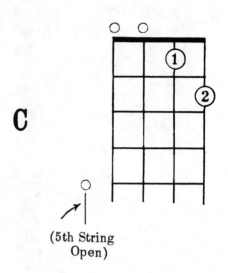

C

(5th String
Open)

**Do not place fingers on the frets but
directly behind them.**

Do not apply too much pressure.

Practice the above Chord until the tone is clear.

/ / / / = Strokes of the Pick over the Strings.

/ / / = Strum the C chord three times in succession.

TIME SIGNATURES

$\frac{4}{4}$ or C = COMMON TIME

Hold the C chord and play it in this manner:

C	C	C	C

$\frac{4}{4}$ / / / /   / / / /   / / / /   / / /

$\frac{3}{4}$ = THREE-FOUR or WALTZ TIME

Hold the C chord and play it in the following manner:

C	C	C	C

$\frac{3}{4}$ / / /   / / /   / / /   / / /

$\frac{2}{4}$ = TWO-FOUR TIME

Play it in this manner:

C

$\frac{2}{4}$ / /   / /   / /   / /

THE G7 CHORD

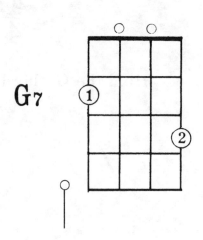

G7

Play the C and G7 chords in the
following manner:

| C | C | G7 | G7 |

$\frac{4}{4}$ / / / /   / / / /   / / / /   / / / /

| C | G7 | C | G7 |

/ / / /   / / / /   / / / /   / / / /

| C | G7 | C | G7 | C | G7 | C |

/ / / /   / / / /   / / /   𝄽 / 𝄽

←REST→

𝄽 = Rest.   It indicates a period of silence.

**See ''BANJO CHORDS''
by MEL BAY**

OUR FIRST SONG
(Using the C and G7 Chords)

Long, Long Ago

Be sure to play the
chords directly on each word or
syllable as indicated.

Down In The Valley

* Continue playing the C chord until you reach the G7 chord.
  Play G7 until you arrive at C.

Skip To My Lou

* No chord strokes on words in parenthesis ( ).

Buffalo Gals

Oh, My Darling Clementine

There will be no playing on the pick-up notes
at the beginning of the above song.

For additional Chord Studies,

See ''BANJO CHORDS''
by MEL BAY

THE "F" CHORD

F

Master the following Chord Study:

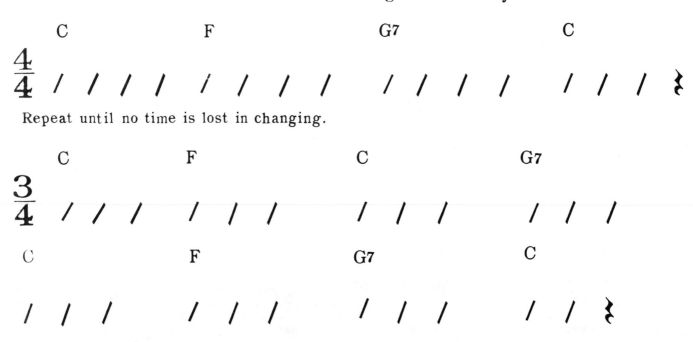

The C, F and G7 chords are the principal chords in the Key of C.

See "BANJO CHORDS"
by MEL BAY

The Blue Tail Fly

* ⌒ = Hold the note extra long as in a pause.

**See ''BANJO CHORDS''
by MEL BAY**

On Top Of Old Smoky

The Marines Hymn

There Is A Tavern In The Town

* The Pick-up note may be played by striking the third string open.

* Strum the pick over the chord slowly
as in a harp style and let it ring.

THE D7 CHORD

D7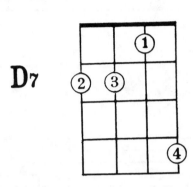

Play the following Chord Study:

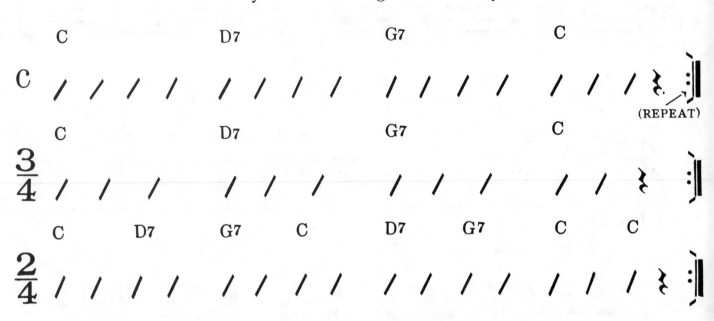

Master the above study before proceeding.

For supplementary chord studies,

See "BANJO CHORDS"
by MEL BAY

Our Boys Will Shine Tonight

(Introducing the D7 Chord)

In the last measure play the bass note on the first beat,
rest and play the C chord on the third beat.
The fourth beat is silent.

THE G CHORD

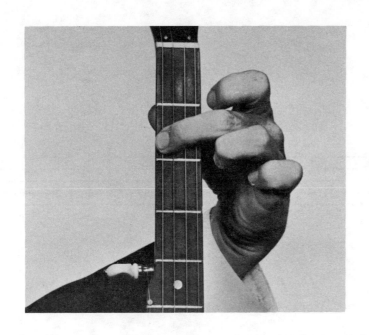

G

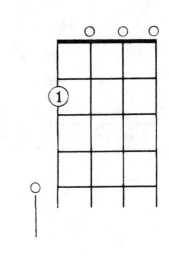

The chords in the Key of G are: G, C and D7.

Play the following Chord Study:

G	C	D7	G

$\frac{4}{4}$ / / / / / / / / / / / / / / / ≹]|

G	G7	C	D7

$\frac{4}{4}$ / / / / / / / / / / / / / / / /

G	D7	G	G

/ / / / / / / / / / / / / / / ≹]|

See "BANJO CHORDS"
by MEL BAY

The Old Grey Mare

**For follow-up chord and strum techniques,
see FUN WITH STRUMS — BANJO**

She'll Be Coming Round The Mountain

Hand Me Down My Walking Cane

In order to start your song in the correct key,
strum the principal chord lightly before beginning.
In the above song the principal or tonic chord is G.

Red River Valley

SOME MORE CHORDS

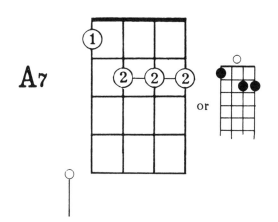

A7

or

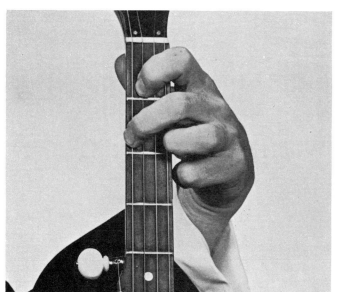

E7

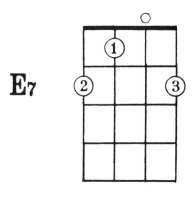

B7

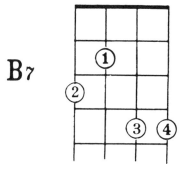

FUN WITH CHORDS IN "C"

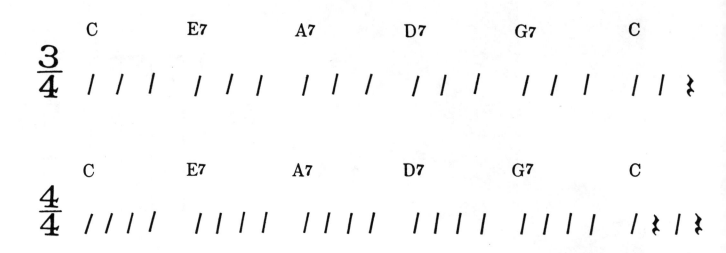

MORE FUN WITH CHORDS IN "G"

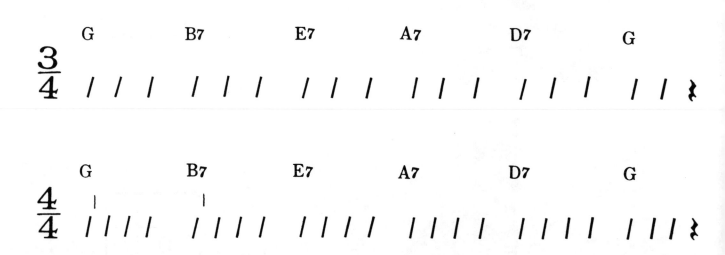

See "BANJO CHORDS"
by MEL BAY

Home on The Range

I've Been Working On The Railroad

32

In The Evening By The Moonlight

In the above song
strum the chords slowly.

THE D CHORD

D

D	G	A7	D

$\frac{4}{4}$ / / / /   / / / /   / / / /   / / / /

D	G	A7	D

$\frac{3}{4}$ / / /   / / /   / / /   / / ⸒

D	B7	E7	A7

$\frac{4}{4}$ / / / /   / / / /   / / / /   / / / /

D	D7	G	D

/ / / /   / / / /   / / / /   / / / ⸒

Darling Nellie Gray

My Bonnie

Little Annie Rooney

Oh! Susanna

Good Night Ladies

SUMMARY
The Major Chords
Each Form must be thoroughly mastered before proceeding to the next.

I

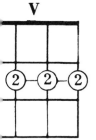

Frets	1	2	3	4	5	6	7	8	9	10	11	12	13
Chords	F	F#/Gb	G	Ab	A	Bb	B	C	Db/C#	D	Eb	E	F

III

Frets	1	2	3	4	5	6	7	8	9	10	11	12	13
Chords	Db/C#	D	Eb	E	F	Gb/F#	G	Ab	A	Bb	B	C	Db/C#

V

Frets	1	2	3	4	5	6	7	8	9	10	11	12	13
Chords	A	Bb	B	C	Db/C#	D	Eb	E	F	Gb/F#	G	Ab	A

The Minor Chords

Im

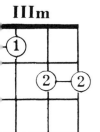

Frets	1	2	3	4	5	6	7	8	9	10	11	12	13
Chords	Fm	Gbm/F#m	Gm	Abm	Am	Bbm	Bm	Cm	Dbm/C#m	Dm	Ebm	Em	Fm

IIIm

Frets	1	2	3	4	5	6	7	8	9	10	11	12	13
Chords	Dbm/C#m	Dm	Ebm	Em	Fm	Gbm/F#m	Gm	Abm	Am	Bbm	Bm	Cm	Dbm/C#m

Vm

Frets	1	2	3	4	5	6	7	8	9	10	11	12	13
Chords	Am	Bbm	Bm	C	Dbm/C#m	Dm	Ebm	Em	Fm	Gbm/F#m	Gm	Abm	Am

THE SEVENTH CHORDS

I^7

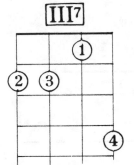

Frets	1	2	3	4	5	6	7	8	9	10	11	12
Chords	F7	Gb7 F#7	G7	Ab7	A7	Bb7	B7	C7	Db7 C#7	D7	Eb7	E7

III^7

Frets	1	2	3	4	5	6	7	8	9	10	11	12
Chords	D7	Eb7	E7	F7	Gb7 F#7	G7	Ab7	A7	Bb7	B7	C7	Db7 C#7

V^7

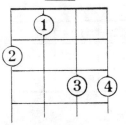

Frets	1	2	3	4	5	6	7	8	9	10	11	12
Chords	Bb7	B7	C7	Db7 C#7	D7	Eb7	E7	F7	Gb7 F#7	G7	Ab7	A7

VII^7

Frets	1	2	3	4	5	6	7	8	9	10	11	12
Chords	Ab7	A7	Bb7	B7	C7	Db7 C#7	D7	Eb7	E7	F7	Gb7 F#7	G7

For a maximum collection of etudes for chord progressions and study, employ the etudes found in the "MEL BAY CHORD SYSTEM" for the modern orchestral guitar.

For follow-up chord and strum techniques, see FUN WITH STRUMS — BANJO